NORFOLK IN A NUTSHELL

Further details of Poppyland Publishing titles can be found at
www.poppyland.co.uk
*where clicking on the 'Support and Resources' button
will lead to pages specially compiled to support this book*

Join us for more Norfolk and Suffolk stories and background at
www.facebook.com/poppylandpublishing

and follow **@poppylandpub**

Norfolk in a Nutshell

KEITH SKIPPER

POPPYLAND
PUBLISHING

First published 2014 by Poppyland Publishing, Cromer, NR27 9AN
www.poppyland.co.uk

ISBN 978 1 909796 12 6

Designed and typeset in 12 on 14.4 pt Gilgamesh
Printed by Lightning Source

DEDICATION

Dedicated to all who nod their heads in approval on reading this stirring testimonial:

"The Norfolk man is a hard one to move. He would rather starve in Norfolk than grow fat in London. When he has made up his mind you can't move him farther than you can swing a bullock by its tail. And that's not far." — King's Lynn man explaining why Lynn dockers wouldn't go to London for work.
Norfolk Journal, January, 1915

All-round praise

Evidently from the pen of a Norfolk man, but from general report it is not very far from the truth ... "Whether we survey the county with regard to the climate, population, commerce, the character of the inhabitants, its diversified beauties or the improved state of its agriculture, it may with propriety be termed the glory of England."

Rev Benjamin Armstrong, *Norfolk Diary,* 1850

FOREWARNED

By Granny Biffin, by a country mile Bronickle End's oldest and wisest indigenous remnant.

This is the first time I have been asked to set the scene for a book about my beloved Norfolk. I suspect it will be the last as I approach the sort of three figures designed to send any village cricket batsman into rhapsodies.

Let me make it abundantly clear from the start that this is not your usual "Welcome to the best place on earth" guide for newcomers and tourists. Nor is it a "Let's pull up the drawbridge and keep the beggars out!" manual for hardened and cynical natives.

No, it's a totally unfashionable attempt to be brutally honest and straightforward about a blessed plot subjected to wild rumours and extreme verdicts ever since I was a little mawther with pigtails dangling over my floral pinafore.

I well remember Great Aunt Phoebe from somewhere in fashionable Middlesex on holiday with us in the 1920s exclaiming "Oh, no, not more dratted cows and mucky sugar beet! Take me home to civilisation!"

I also recall a cousin from London evacuated to live with us out in the sticks during the last war rushing up to a neighbouring farmer and shouting "Quick, mister, come an' see ... the 'orse is losing 'is petrol!"

Mr Skipper, all too often a prophet without honour in his own parish, could have sought the services of some transient celebrity or an old friend in high places to introduce his latest tome.

But he has persuaded me to "come out of the closet" at the bottom of my country cottage garden to prove he is not alone in a totally honourable campaign to stop dear old Norfolk from being sold short.

We are kindred spirits. We want Norfolk to be appreciated more for the right reasons, not continually exploited for all the wrong ones.

We want our home county to retain something of its unique character while accepting a few small changes may be for the better. Like electric lights, mains sewerage and that Skype thingy I can use to mardle with my great-grandson Rupert in New York.

I am truly flattered to be invited to bang the drum for such a challenging volume, accepting as a reward two bottles of home-made rhubarb wine and a charabanc ride to Cromer Pier on my milestone birthday.

Here's *Norfolk in a Nutshell*. Crack it open and share the unfading delights.

Stirring events

Never be ashamed of the dialect and customs of good old Norfolk. If we are behind the times compared with other counties, we can console ourselves with the thoughts that Norfolk men have played their part, and that right well, in the stirring events of our nation's history.

Walton N Dew, *A Dyshe of Norfolk Dumplings*, 1896

Contents

1. Origins

Where did Norfolk come from? Some would say that's easier to answer than working out where it might be going as the 21st century gathers pace.

Biggest concern about the future must be Norfolk's chances of maintaining a strong identity and flavour of its own against a murky tide of uniformity and "do-as-you're-told" instructions from bland politicians at all levels held to ransom by big business and the money gods.

Fondest hopes should be based on unyielding geographical features spelling glorious isolation when needed from the rest of Britain. That defiant posterior sticking out into the Old German Ocean makes the point emphatically. What is viewed by too many as Norfolk's biggest weakness can turn out to be its biggest strength.

Writer and broadcaster James Wentworth Day proclaimed in the 1970s: "If the rest of Britain sank beneath the waves, and Norfolk was left alone, islanded in the turmoil of the seas, it would, I think, survive without too much trouble ... Norfolk has always stood alone and aloof from the rest of England."

In fact, those who were there to jot down impressions at the very beginning of man's history tell us much of the North Sea (trendy new name for Old German Ocean) and the Fens were dry land and Britain was part of Europe. That's well before Norfolk was entirely covered by ice and doubts about where to build its first incinerator in the event of warming up again.

Apparently it wasn't until 7,000 – 6,000 BC that the rising sea level finally cut the land link between Britain and Europe and Norfolk covered a much larger area than at any time since.

So emerged the climate of independence and cussedness pitched against a multitude of marauding invaders who thought the natives would be so grateful for helping hands along the road to true progress...

Of course, it couldn't have been as simple as that. New evidence has come to light, not only to discredit the rather naive assertion that the county's name is merely a shortening of "North folk" (as distinct from that rum lot squatting under the banner of "South folk"), but also to lay claim to far more elevated connections.

We can dispense immediately with puckish ideas that an Iceni tribal tendency to "gnaw folk" during the Roman invasion has anything to do with the christening of our proud homeland. Queen Boadicea and her warriors were far more interested in mowing down legionaries via flashing blades on chariot wheels than getting their teeth into a vital slice of history.

The same goes for a more recent inference that newcomers and holidaymakers finding it hard to pierce the famous caution and reserve of the locals claimed loudly they "ignore folk ...", an accusation too easily transformed into a telling little label.

No, significant word has come from on high that the real derivation of this fine old county is "Noahfolk", proving we are all descended in a direct line from that great navigator and explorer who was floating his stock while everyone else was in liquidation. And he invented floodlights into the bargain.

Biblical scholars with Norfolk roots point excitedly to Noah's conversation with his son Japheth during an anxious moment in the Ark. "Boy!" boomed Noah, "Hev that mucky ole pidgin come back yit?" Japheth replied, "Noo, faather, that hent, not yit that hent." Noah's other sons, Ham and Shem, were busy learning to count.

For even stronger confirmation that God Himself is a Norfolk man — or at least a Carrow Road season ticket holder when games are not staged on Sundays — we need look no further than a homely version of the Creation by local Methodist minister, Colin Riches.

He gave several well-known Bible stories a coat of Norfolk paint. While other scribes before him settled for the traditional line "Let there be light", Colin's version, full of parochial power, turned gloriously into the powerful invocation "Le's hev some loight on the job!"

Steady progress.

Slow but sure

A first visit to Norfolk is, I venture to say, a surprise. This county unfolds itself bit by bit as one of the least spoiled districts in England. Its people, its architecture, its customs, its scenery are distinct and individual. It is still geographically an island. It is separated from Suffolk by the Rivers Waveney and Little Ouse and from Cambridgeshire by the Ouse and the Nene. Its eastbound boundary is the North Sea, which beats itself along the ninety miles of the Norfolk coastline. This peculiarity is, no doubt, in some measure responsible for the individuality of Norfolk. You feel when in Norfolk that you are in a country, not a county.

H V Morton, *The Land of the Vikings*, 1928

2. ROMANS

True Norfolk defenders have remained mightily suspicious about changes dressed up as progress ever since that crafty reprobate Maximus Secondhomeicus launched his Best-Crept Pillage Competition for posh visitors a few centuries ago.

We are told the fearsome Roman army of occupation had gone by 420, a clear indication they didn't fancy being caught up in rush-hour traffic largely of their own making. It had more than doubled by 430 AD (Approaching Deadlock).

New roads, new towns, new industries, booming economic and social development ... mission accomplished! So much better than Norfolk BC (Broadband Coming). The invaders could pack their togas, helmets and dialect phrase-books after a few farewell cheese-and-mead parties and move on to enlighten other musty corners across the globe.

It was missionary work with perks on an industrial scale and set the tone for so many others intent on dragging Norfolk out of the Dark Ages by giving them things already mucking up places from which their would-be saviours had escaped in earnest droves.

As one old Norfolk boy mused recently as he sipped a pint of mild in the snug of The Eradicated Coypu, "Thass bin a'gorn on since time immoral."

Of course, the majority of people in Roman Norfolk were small farmers leading useful lives either in villages or isolated farmsteads. Peasants were apt to mardle fondly about the good old days when you could get a grandstand seat for a spot of sacking, burning and looting and cheer "that mawther Boodiker" as she hossed past in her chariot on the way to another important battle or W l (Wild Iceni) meeting.

There were persistent rumours of rampant anti-social behaviour on day outings to Camulodunum, Verulamium and Londinium (later to be known as Colchester, St Albans and The Smoke) but those phlegmatic sons and daughters of the soil knew it was best to keep their noses out of matters that didn't immediately concern them.

They did encounter one Roman soldier seeking strawfloor-and-breakfast on his way to Fenland to weigh up salt production, an important local industry destined to become an imperial monopoly.

This soldier refused to give his name and number for security reasons. His hosts at Dundiggin (three stars, all visible through the roof) dubbed him Sorftewlicus and passed on condiments of the season.

Evening classes in pottery, spinning, weaving, tax levies, map reading and foreign languages were sponsored by building contractors Daub & Wattle in areas with growing populations, especially after the town of Venta Icenorum sprang from the pastures of what we now know as Caistor St Edmund, a few miles from Norwich.

This is not to be confused with Caister-on-Sea, a new port founded by the Romans near the mouth of the Yare in readiness for importing holidaymakers, hessian nightshirts, Scottish fishergirls and offshore wind experts.

It was a shrewd move by developers keen on bare-faced bribery (now known as planning gain) to include in the new town's name some sort of tribute to the Iceni tribe once so prominent in these parts before being put to the sword. Even so, proposals for a Boadicea Bistro and Woad Safety Information Centre in the stone forum were turned down by licensing authorities.

There is some evidence Venta Icenorum had both a water supply and a sewerage system. A bath house proved particularly popular among casually-dressed tourists later revealed to be early Saxon spies on their way to Sutton Who for a chariot boat sale — original version of the car boot extravaganza.

The Romans, of course, were determined to underline the importance of new roads, not least to help them get out of certain locations in a hurry when colonial benevolence might not be fully appreciated. Their hasty retreat from trying to gatecrash a ploughing match at Oxwick claims a colourful chapter in local folklore.

Perhaps the Pedallers' Way was their most ambitious project, linking north Essex with the Wash and Lincolnshire. It failed only because their patent for a wooden bicycle got lost in the post. At least that's what that lot up in Londinium said.

Venta Icenorum Town Senate's Infrastructure Policy Sub-committee spent a host of fractious hours discussing the merits or otherwise of street lighting on the edge of town before permanent fortifications could be built. The local paper, The Taciturn Tablet, revelled in "Roman in the gloamin'" headlines.

One of their guest columnists, Ringroadicus, constantly chided "blinkered sections of the population who set up ludicrous barriers in the way of glorious tomorrows". He also demonstrated a remarkable gift for seeing into the future when he urged all readers to "keep on taking The Tablet and back the NDR campaign."

The fact he was referring not to the Northern Distributor Road but to the Never Doubt Romans philosophy should not detract from what he and his colleagues did for us.

Independence

Norfolk villages convey, if not a sense of the picturesque, a beauty born of a thousand years of life, a millennium of man's eternal struggle. It is a far more deeply felt beauty than the superficial. It changes much across the fourth largest county of England. Below South Lopham where the River Waveney almost meets the River Little Ouse, and a single thin sliver of road joins Norfolk to the rest of England, there is the same feeling of independence as there is on Mundesley beach. To watch the sun set in the sea at Dersingham or Snettisham and rise again at Sea Palling or Caister is to experience a feeling that this independence matters.

David Kennett, *Norfolk Villages*, 1980

3. HISTORY

They say history is written by the winners. Well, I wasn't there for a lot of it and so I'm prone to adopt a reasonable Norfolk stance and treat it all with a degree of scepticism.

In moments of high fantasy I nip in when no-one's looking to alter a few things, mainly for the better. Like changing "Turnip" Townshend into "Turnup" Townshend and crediting him with the introduction of proper trousers for workers on the Raynham estate.

Thomas Coke of Holkham followed that sort of pioneering spirit when he championed sheep-sharings, a bright idea destined to spill over into a golden age of co-operative farming.

Both luminaries loved their grub and may well have influenced the Norfolk Four-Course Menu at Carrow Road and other gourmet establishments.

This must not be confused with outstanding community work in the Melton Constable area in the early 1800s when a quartet of trailblazing law enforcers took it in turns to stamp out villainy in the worst-affected villages.

The Norfolk Four-Cop Rotation system won many admirers long before Robert Peel craftily stole the idea to sort out a London police force. He sent men out in pairs to save money.

Talking of capital gains in the Norfolk colonies, would our beloved Chelsea-on-Sea ever have emerged if Horatio Nelson had first seen light of day at Barton Bendish rather than Burnham Thorpe?

It's not too difficult to imagine well-heeled stars of stage, screen and ravioli touching down at nearby RAF Marham in readiness for a cosy

Sheep-sharings at Holkham?

weekend among the genteel folk of Mayfair-at-Ease around the unspoilt charms of Barton Bendish, Beachamwell, Boughton and Bexwell.

What if the Danes and Vikings had left their rape and silage behind when they called to see how our mobile phone signal was coming on? Had they concentrated instead on encouraging the noble art of dwile flonking we might now well be anticipating the mining of even more gold at the next Olympic Games.

What if Robert Kett and his rebellions chums had won the Battle of Dussindale in 1549? Would that large housing development north of Norwich have received planning permission?

What if Clement Scott had got as far as Bacton on his clifftop ramble after arriving in Cromer by train in 1883 and finding the place packed out? Would he have weighed up prospects for natural gas ahead of an unnatural pipeline to London's Victorian yuppies?

If Norwich mawther Sarah Glover had not invented the Tonic-Sol-Fa system in the 1800s, would we have been spared the boasts of people who went to see the film Sound of Music over 200 times?

If William Faden hadn't published what is believed to be the first large-scale map of Norfolk on August 12th, 1797, would new drivers in the county have better excuses for getting lost and blaming the locals for turning signposts round?

What if Norwich City had beaten Luton Town in their FA Cup semi-final replay and gone on to lift the old trophy in 1959? Would it have been Sir Archie Macauley tasting World Cup glory with England in 1966 instead of that chap who did a useful job at Ipswich?

What if King's Lynn and Thetford had rejected expansion schemes actively encouraged by London overspill supporters in the 1960s? Would they be more appealing places in which to live and work as a result of not heeding siren voices?

What if all those people violently opposed to the introduction of wheelie bins a few years back had got their way? Would civilisation as we know, love and recycle it have been left lying in a state to mock Norfolk's growing green reputation?

Tantalising questions to suggest some old codgers stuck in their homely ways found plenty to moan about when the Romans arrived to cheer up the peasants through the good offices of their lawyers, Sacking, Burning & Looting.

Flint towers

Church towers dominate the Norfolk countryside. From any point of vantage, the gentle unemphatic landscape of farmland and woodland rolls away, mile after mile, to the dim horizons of the sea. Slowly and subtly the colours change with the seasons and the crops; corn and roots, stubble and ploughland, olland and pasture, gorse and bracken, the beechwoods and the ash-carrs and the oaks in the hedgerows, all contribute to build up a scene which unceasingly alters as the months go by. Unchanged against this ever-varying background of colour stand the grey flint towers rising in every village above cottage roofs or from groups of ancient trees. Each tower represents many centuries of history; it stood there before the cottages and the trees, and it will outlast them, an emblem of the continuity of English life.

R W Ketton-Cremer, *A Norfolk Gallery*, 1948

4. HOLIDAYS

Countryside writer Edward Thomas, weighing up the glories of high summer in 1906, gently sighed: "We are so rich that we do not count our treasure."

A typically poetic turn of phrase worth pinning at the top of our August calendars as we grouse about traffic, trippers, sunburn, soakings, noise, nettles and crawling nasties – and take all the good things for granted.

It's the main holiday month, shorthand for rigorous examination of tolerance levels in family and community where varying interests and ages tug in different directions.

One man's carnival is another man's cacophony. One woman's shopping is another woman's shudder. One child's cry of boredom is enough to inspire cosy thoughts of a new school year and getting late earlier.

Now, when I was a lad and harvest holidays beckoned, we had the good sense to go into virtual exile for a few blissful weeks. Parents saw us off early in the morning with sandwiches and a bottle of cold tea and then provided soap and water for tired, dirty bodies as the dusk trumpet sounded.

Such freedom could come at a price. Picking fruit and carting corn can turn tedious after a while but we relished the trust invested in us to follow the country code and to honour the family name. We knew the grim consequences of failing either.

Perhaps our social climate and holiday habits have changed too much to regard all that as anything but simple Norfolk nostalgia. Even

so, a chance to catch a whiff of independence ought to remain one of the most useful by-products of a long summer break.

I popped into Norfolk's least trendy pub, the Dewdrop Inn at Lower Dodman, to compare notes with that ever-youthful trio of indigenous icons, retired coypu catcher Ernie Hoskins, retired stack thatcher Horry Barnes and retired muck spreader Billy Archer.

They aim to ride out the worst of any lingering recession on a wave of old-fashioned community spirit and mild beer while saving up to £20,000 apiece to guarantee basic social care and support when they really need it.

Some luxuries have been sacrificed already. All three gave the most recent Latitude Festival a miss "because foreign travel is simply too expensive" and the pub's annual mystery tour to Egmere has been put on hold until December.

"I've never known anything like it" said Ernie Hoskins. "Each year it grows harder to make ends meet." He was referring to his hands and feet.

"I'm refusing to get downhearted" said Horry Barnes. "I still don't need glasses." He drinks straight from the bottle.

"I have to take a pill every day for the rest of my life" said Billy Archer. "It worries me no end." The doctor only gave him four.

I asked what they missed most about those good old days in Norfolk when low wages, modest expectations and high regard for the home-rule mantra gave the county a glow of contentment.

"Catching coypu" said Ernie Hoskins.

"Thatching stacks" said Horry Barnes.

"Spreading muck" said Billy Archer.

"And why do they call it Norwich North? We don't say Raynham West, Pickenham South, Tuddenham East or Dodman Lower" opined mine host Jason Bullard, anxious to show important views are still on tap.

That gave Ernie Hoskins time to brew up a more erudite answer as he unwrapped Spam sandwiches from a frayed fourses bag.

"When I was young I wanted to be master of my fate and captain of my soul. Now I'll settle for being master of my weight and captain of

Opposite: *Fourses under the hedge.*

the darts team."

A clear pitch for votes at the September annual meeting. He passed round sandwiches with a knowing wink that could have meant they were covered by expenses.

Enter the vicar, the Rev Jacob "Billy" Windham, like a phantom returning officer ready to declare a number of newly-saved souls on his register.

He looked after St Walstan's in Lower Dodman and eight other churches in the Puckaterry Parva group. "In the midst of life we are in debt" he offered as a small affront to the "no texting" sign over the bar.

He was hosting the first monthly Dewdrop Inn Debate while fiscal pressures persisted. "I've chosen my subject for Sunday's sermon" he declared. "It concerns the retired coypu catcher who surprised both God and his humble earthly representative in this parish when he dropped a fiver on the collection plate ..."

Sandwich munching ceased. ".... and was asked if this was a donation or an investment. Priceless, what?"

Beyond criticism

I have just returned from a weekend in Norfolk. From the conversation at the dinner table on the first evening I gathered that my great crime against Norfolk is that I, a mere Southerner, have dared to criticise this county in any way whatsoever. Apparently, Norfolk is beyond criticism. Norfolk is a farming county. There one talks farming, thinks farming, dreams farming, and lives farming, almost to the exclusion of all else; but the only farming which is considered worthy of notice is the type of farming which has been carried on in Norfolk since time immemorial. Change — any change — even a change for the better — is regretted.

A G Street, *Country Calendar*, 1935

5. DIFFERENT

Norfolk has plenty in common with Cornwall beyond an isolation bequeathed by geography that has shaped character and worked hard to protect it.

Nelson's County sticks its sturdy backside into the Old German Ocean while the land of the pasty and clotted cream dangles its feet in the Atlantic as if at a first rehearsal for pulling away from Britain altogether.

Both prize vibrant dialects confused and ridiculed in equal measure by graduates from Mummerzet House, finishing school for all-purpose yokelspeak so beloved of national television and radio producers.

Both sample the mixed blessings of tourist charabancs in full cry and an unfair sprinkling of second homes where locals are locked out by ridiculous house prices. The Cornish Riviera is nearly as posh as Chelsea-on-Sea, that well-heeled colony built around Burnham Market.

Cornwall has King Arthur and Merlin. Norfolk has Queen Boadicea and The Singing Postman. They have piskies and old tin mines. We have Black Shuck and Grimes Graves. They have Daphne du Maurier and William Golding. We have Mary Mann and Malcolm Bradbury.

Both counties have just one city — take a bow Truro and Norwich — and share a proud reputation for valuing and defending distinctiveness. However, our friends in the west appear to have stolen a big march on the route to independence.

The Cornish have been officially recognised as a national minority along with the Scots, Welsh and Irish. It's a handsome victory for campaigners who have long insisted that beyond all the touristy images packaged so neatly the county has a distinct language and culture worthy of formal recognition.

The status of a national minority group, made under a European convention to protect them, means the Cornish have the same rights and safeguards as more established members of Britain's Celtic fringe.

A long battle to assert a special individual identity took a significant turn when 84,000 people declared themselves "Cornish" in the 2011 Census following a campaign for that designation to be added to the form.

A further 41 per cent of pupils in Cornwall's schools described themselves as Cornish in a 2011 school survey — up from 34 per cent two years earlier. The Cornish language, which until 2010 was classified as extinct by UNESCO, is enjoying a robust revival with over 500 people claiming the Celtic dialect as their main language. There's even a Cornish language crèche.

Dual-language street signs are now common throughout the county. Its three Liberal Democrat MPs swore their oath in Cornish when elected to Parliament in 2010.

I have long advocated that all those seeking seats in Westminster in Norfolk's name should live in the county for five years at least to fully acclimatise themselves with special needs of a very special place. And how uplifting it would be to hear even the slightest tincture of a real Norfolk voice rise above the din at Prime Minister's Question Time!

We may have to wait for the first Norfolk-born Speaker of the House of the modern era before timely instructions like "Howld yar slarver!" and "Will yew stop hallerin'!" restore a semblance of sanity to proceedings.

Norfolk-flavoured road signs could well move on from well-established favourites like "Slow Yew Down "and "Missin' Signpust Ahead" to more subtle offerings such as "Honk if you meet a herd o'cows" and "Why ent yew usin' the park-an'-ride?". Dialect is a useful vehicle to kick-start a bandwagon.

Norfolk, I expect, will take a customary in-depth look at all implications before raising the standard bearing a ferret rampant over rusting concrete mixer and emphasising yet again that true local identity must always stay ahead of regional ineptitude, national ideology and global idealism. "Dew diffrunt" ought to be able to embrace self-determination.

Of course, most constitutional experts will dismiss this Cornish uprising as no more than a spot of home-made fun rather than the start of the Balkanisation of the United Kingdom.

Even, so there have been several calls for similar status from other counties. One of the most persuasive is a demand for Hampshire independence "because there are more of us than in Cornwall and we are very different from Surrey."

A Yorkshire declaration is expected soon ... although the thought of Geoffrey Boycott being installed as emperor with a stick of rhubarb in one hand and a microphone in the other does beg far more important questions than it answers.

'Dreadful place'

A cousin of mine arrived with the following amusing sidelight on the Norfolk character. At a recent London luncheon party she found herself sitting next to a distinguished American lady who had to flee the country because of threats to kidnap her daughter. She was anxiously discussing in what part of England she should buy a house and settle. After having run through the advantages of various counties she concluded: "Of course, I did think of Norfolk, but believe me a friend of mine said 'My dear, never go there. It's a dreadful place; I assure you no-one in Norfolk ever calls till the third generation!' "

Lilias Rider Haggard, *Norfolk Life*, 1943

Things they never said

"Very hilly, Norfolk" — *Noel Coward*

"Give me a nice nut roast any day" — *Bernard Matthews*

"You won't get me out on a night like this" — *Henry Blogg*

"Think I'll take the bus" — *Will Kemp*

"I find these Romans so civilised" — *Queen Boadicea*

"London? You wait until I get my hands on that Roman that lent me the sat-nav for this chariot! " — Boadicea

"On the whole I preferred Brancaster and the Creakes" — *Lord Nelson*

"I did it all without a visa" — *Tom Paine*

"I still visit Blickling regularly" — *Anne Boleyn*

"I'm not that keen on it myself" — *Jeremiah Colman*

"My initials came in handy" — *Henry Rider Haggard*

"Let's call it Square Table" — *Louis Marchesi*

"I'll keep quiet about this beautiful area" — *Clement Scott*

"Just a small salad for tea" — *Parson Woodforde*

Clement Scott in later life — regretting Bungalowland.

"I wish they'd give it to someone else" — *Percy Varco*

"One of my songs carries a Government Health Warning" — *Singing Postman*

"Nothing of real interest in here" — Howard Carter.

" You can't beat a good laugh" — *William Cowper.*

"Can't stand those creepy-crawlies " — *Ted Ellis.*

"Much quicker by email" — *Margaret Paston.*

"I'm not the political type" — *Luke Hansard.*

6. DIALECT

It has to be one of the heaviest burdens any gnarled old Norfolk native is destined to bear ... a strong suspicion that he's being patronised or pitied.

I ought to be used to it by now after years of ploughing unfashionable furrows and regularly accepting the role of anachronism in a modern media world along the international information super-highway.

Why on earth should anyone prefer to get stuck down a hemlock-choked country lane exchanging droll yarns, dialect phrases and dogmatic points of view? What's the attraction in being hailed a quaint left-over from an idyllic pastoral scene that might not have existed after all?

There can be scope for critics and cynics to admit it may be nice to see people building their own village halls, reviving that old-fashioned community spirit and trying to hold on to pubs, buses, hedgerows and local colour. The art of condescension is not yet dead. But when it comes to that very peculiar dialect...

My customary response centres on Norfolk's exceptional powers of absorption. The old place still permits a parochial renegade not only the right to exist with impunity but also to flourish without apology in a climate where "dew diffrunt" sunshine bursts mercifully through dull clouds of uniformity.

I take fresh courage when needed from champions of the vernacular with a disarming habit of bringing it into play to confuse or confound

Opposite: *Eric Fowler, doyen of dialect at the* Eastern Daily Press, *discusses the Thetford vineyard vintage.*

Troshin' Time.

the opposition. Many a scullery maid cursed a dowager and lived to savour the tale. The odd serf must have damned his feudal landlord and been allowed to keep his chains.

Dark mutterings in dialect have been interpreted by new village parsons as welcome signs of repentance among dwindling flocks. Schoolteachers are not immune. I heard of one pre-Ofsted luminary who gave a pupil top marks after being informed "Yew duzzy ole fewl!" was a pre-Chaucer greeting and one small strand in a glorious and colourful heritage.

Swearing in broad Norfolk, hardly encouraged but still a potent weapon in the underdog's armoury, carries an almost lyrical ring. And if you smile while in full cry, chances are the target will consider it some kind of ancient blessing.

In short, our dialect can bring vital balance to one-sided situations and lend much-needed perspective when life gets too complicated, too fast and too serious. Take two rural sages mardling about the merits or otherwise of making the A11 a dual carriageway:

"Carnt see much sense innit mesself" said the first old boy. "Thousands more hossin' inter Norfolk cors that'll be a rare lot easier ter git here ..."

His friend thought for a whole minute. Then he beamed, "Ah, so they might ... but that dew mean they'll clear orff quicker anorl!"

It may continue to suffer from dilution and will have to adapt to stay afloat in some areas. National television and wireless dramas seem more than likely to carry on sinking in murky Mummerzet waters. But the dialect is simply too strong and too precious to let go.

Max Müller, the German-born writer who lived and studied in Britain for most of his life, waved a highly influential flag for the cause well over a century ago when he informed Eastern Daily Press readers: "The real and natural life of language is in its dialects.

"Even in England the local patois have many forms which are more primitive than the language of Shakespeare, and the richness of their vocabulary surpasses on many points that of the classical writer of any period."

Perhaps my old friend and mentor Eric Fowler, who wrote with such style and distinction for the Eastern Daily Press as Jonathan Mardle, issued the most defiant call to arms worthy of an encore whenever someone is misguided enough to suggest dialect's days are surely numbered:

"I would like true Norfolk to survive because of its expressive vocabulary and vivid turn of phrase — so much more vigorous (and honest) than the gobbledegook of the bureaucrats and sociologists with which we are nowadays so smothered that the language itself is in danger of losing its meaning.

"The English country dialects, if they do indeed remain alive, may well become the last repository — outside of old books — of good plain English."

Settle down

It is a fact that after a "foreigner" has lived 20 years in the county, he is still a new arrival; he may, however, be accepted by that time as the kind of new arrival who will be made welcome if he cares to settle down.

Doreen Wallace, *Norfolk*, 1951

Character test

You are entitled to be called a true Norfolk character when..........

- You learnt to drive on a field or disused aerodrome.

- Your car has mud and straw in the boot.

- You use more than two fingers to wave to tractor drivers met on the road.

- You can sing along to at least five Singing Postman numbers.

- You know how to walk over a cattle grid.

- You know what grockles are.

- You take a torch to the pub.

- You leave it on the counter at closing time.

- You can recite full details of Norwich City's 1958-59 FA Cup Run.

- You know knockin' and toppin' was not an ancient futility rite.

- You like the sound of cockerels crowing early in the morning.

- You can explain what "Dew yew keep a'troshin'!" really means.

7. TOGETHERNESS

My Norfolk country childhood, much more *Rooks and Reprobates* than *Swallows and Amazons*, fashioned an incurable sense of identity and place.

We cherished our patch, defended it when necessary and treated with the utmost suspicion anyone or anything that threatened to upset our carefully constructed applecart.

Tucked away cosily between Dereham and Swaffham, far enough from the noise and speed of the grimly functional A47 to hint at a reasonable impression of Brigadoon, our little parish rooted in the regular rhythms of farms and fields largely ignored the rest of the world.

Of course, such glorious innocence — we like to call it self-sufficiency — could not last. Commuters and well-heeled retired folk seeking pastoral refuge replaced a dwindling land army left scanning headlands for reinforcements that never came. Mechanisation marched in to turn tied cottages into Sunday colour supplement fodder and to push giant horses towards rural museum furrows.

A brutally simplistic summary of what happened after I was demobbed from Eden in the early 1960s. But I am trying hard to avoid tumbling into sentimental traps usually reserved for those who loved and lost. Or even learnt and left.

While looking back with fondness and gratitude on those calm but austere post-war years for giving me a strong set of values to go with that unfading sense of location, I recognise and respect what succeeding generations of country dwellers, including members of my own family,

I'm glad we only have to build the stacks once a year.

have managed to achieve on far thinner resources.

Communities like ours, a fair number of whom might have been blissfully unaware of each other, took school, pub, shop, chapel, church and village hall for granted. Football, cricket and darts teams flourished. There were also enough expert volunteers to keep the roads open when it snowed.

Postal and newspaper deliveries rarely faltered. Bread, groceries, meat, fish, paraffin, bottles of Corona, recharged accumulators and fresh laundry arrived regularly at the door. We grew our own vegetables. Buses called twice a week to widen shopping and social horizons in town. The doctor or district nurse came when you called.

Now I'm on nodding terms with most of Norfolk's 700-odd villages after over half-a-century of regular rounds as chronicler, broadcaster, entertainer and nosy native, I wonder how many can come anywhere close to boasting that list of facilities and services.

Okay, the hunnycart has run out of steam, little shuds down the yard have tumbled into history. The old tin bath in front of an open fire now rusts in peace. Rural life can be wholly comfortable, even posh for those who bring adequate resources from big-city adventures.

Even so, I suspect our rough-and-ready era fostered a spirit of togetherness current politicians would die for, a brand way beyond the scope of arrogant newcomers determined to preach and impose rather than listen and muck in. That is the most common complaint heard on my Norfolk travels.

It's a big county defying one to keep in constant touch with all corners, even in this age of speed and mobility. It seems the coast can claim attention at any time of the year while scores of inland villages hardly ever see a stranger let alone an old friend.

Sport continues to build and maintain a host of local bridges with enthusiasts piling into other neighbourhoods, often for the first time as a result of promotion or relegation. Women's Institutes and other travel-hungry organisations do their bit. Yet it seems strange to assume more people in Ashwellthorpe have been to Ibiza or Malta than to Itteringham and Mileham. Even stranger to suggest the majority would find it hard to pinpoint those Norfolk villages.

I could have settled for Alpington, Ingworth and Matlaske and been fairly sure of a similar number of blank faces. It's the sort of exercise created to push missionary zeal to fresh heights.

I launched the county's first official village twinning project in 1984 when the tiny parish of Ovington, near Watton, formed cheerful links with Bodham, close to Holt. I had relished close social ties with both communities and arranged meetings over the microphone on Radio Norfolk's Dinnertime Show.

Over 20 flag-wavers from Bodham, 40 miles away, arrived by bus at Ovington where their hosts turned on the style with stirring home-made entertainment. Other cultural exchanges and sporting fixtures took shape to emphasise how this sort of get-together could be fun as well as worthwhile.

Many Norfolk places are twinned with locations in Europe or further afield and yet they admit to having no idea about other settlements of similar size in their own county.

Bodham, notorious then for madcap Nights of Squit (how I miss 'em!) and Ovington, similarly getting used to the challenge of mixing native know-how with newcomers' impishness, lit a new lantern to togetherness.

With holiday ambitions squeezed by financial restraints, the take-a-break boom closer to home suggested Vibrant Village Ventures could be the answer in Norfolk.

Don't all go at once. That is what spoils well-known bigger targets from seaside to city centre. Pick a friend or family member with an adventurous streak and try a wander and a wonder in a parish you haven't visited before.

Just beware the Rooks and Reprobates.

Famously difficult

The journey into Norfolk is famously difficult. It's kept that way pour decourager les autres. Things have not changed much since Parson Woodforde's time. Tea on the train is horrible swill. If they feel so inclined drivers bring the trains to a clanking halt at Shenfield or perhaps just outside Diss. If you complain too bitterly then they will tell you that somebody has thrown himself under the wheels of the train and that they are waiting to clear the body and scrub the track. It's all done in order to make you feel ashamed, to oblige you to bear up and take it like a man. They especially like to remind you that you have not paid for your seat at all, but only for the privilege of travelling on one of their trains. The A11, too, is a monstrously inconvenient road, dangerous as well. There's a mist that comes down like the clappers in the hollows of Thetford Forest. People quickly get bored of waiting behind lorries full of sugar beet, not to mention lumbering tractors. They overtake when they can't see a thing.

Just the same, the sight of your first pink-washed farmhouse is worth all the trouble ....

Virginia Gay, *Penelope and Adelina*, 1992

8. COMPULSION

I've been playing a little game for years called Give It a Coat of Norfolk Paint. To be honest, it's more of a compulsion as it invades most of my waking hours.

It all began so innocently when I tuned into self-taught sons of the soil among those hemlock-laced lanes of childhood. They put their own rustic spin on national and international events of great significance.

They knew who to blame for that rumpus over the Sewage Canal in 1956 but couldn't work out why Swaffham figured so little as part of that new Common Market soon after. "Hent they got enuff stalls?"

They realised the Cod War against Iceland might put up the price of fish and chips at all local outlets but refused to accept that the Russians sending a dog into space would do anything to improve the weather. "Barkin' mad, the lot onnem."

Their lyrical corruption of the other language I was being taught at school suggested they needed free electrocution lessons to avoid that new mechanical monster, the concubine harvester, and a roll of Anthrax off the top shelf in the village store. Coronation milk went better with tinned peaches than the evacuated stuff according to semi-skimmed workers.

Even regular church and chapel supporters joined in with details of a new parson being induced before he could celebrate Holy Commotion. This must have given rise to the story of the old churchwarden being asked by a newcomer if they had matins in his place of worship. "No," he replied, "We hev lino right up ter the altar."

Perhaps that golden age of instant rural squitticisms reached some sort of peak when a woman said she wasn't very keen on Walsingham "where they hull that incest about". My personal odyssey soon moved on from wisdom across the headlands to spicing up popular culture with a Norfolk flavour.

The wonderful world of wireless turned me into a keen accumulator of homely programmes that really were the cat's whiskers when it came to a distinctly local sound. I could cram Much Binding in the Marsham, Down Your Weybourne, Dick Barton Turf and Desert Island Diss into one sitting before Brooke at Bedtime. This was years before Round the Horning.

I could cite a growing appreciation of local geography for singing, whistling or humming firm favourites like Blow the Wind Southery, Pennies from Hevingham, Concrete and Cley, Move Over Larling, Anmer Down My Walking Cane and It's a Long Way to Little Snoring.

The arrival of mains electricity had to shoulder the blame for television treats such as Dixon of Docking Green, The Forncett Saga, Take Your Pickenham, All Gasthorpe and Gaiters, No Heydon Place and The Rockland Files.

Easton Enders, Beightonwatch and The Skeyton at Night were among delights to come.

Now I was on a roll, ready to impress anyone who'd listen at grammar school with a list of favourite dramatic productions in rehearsal among Norfolk's seriously cultural set. Cue Weeting for Godot or Waiting for Godwick.

My lines were word perfect ... Scole for Scandal, Chicken Soup with Barney, Fransham Without Tears, The Trowsetrap and The Lady's Not For Burnham.

No reason why William Shakespeare (born at Stratton-on-Strawless) should turn up his educated nose at this valuable exercise. Curtain up on Much Ado About Rougham, The Happy Mawthers of Winfarthing, Bit Dark Over Will's Mother's (The Tempest), The Pedlar of Swaffham (The Merchant of Venice) and All's Well that Bawdeswell.

I yearned for Richard lll to break out in Norfolk dialect with the immortal line "A dickey! A dickey! My kingdom for a dickey, ole partner!" or Hamlet to get his skull round torkin' proper with "Blarst me, poor ole Yorrick! Wunner the best, he wuz, allus a good larf an' full o' squit."

It seemed only right to go from bard to worse when the time came to impress young ladies with invitations to watch films owing more to Wicklewood than Hollywood. Few could resist a back seat to savour Caisterblanca, The Matlaske Falcon, Carrowsell, Paint Your Hunnycart, Yaxham Doodle Dandy, Scroby Dick, The Canary has Landed and One Flew Over the Turkey Shed.

I still fall into old habits of my Norfolk travels — only last week I

Horses and fourses.

had to fight off the urge to revive Only Fools and Horsey and Salle of the Century as we ambled through those delightful parishes — but I prefer to demonstrate a growing maturity in the communications field by reducing a rash of groovy labels to properspeak.

For example, "worst-case scenario" becomes "suffin' bad", "positive feedback" turns into "wholly good", "at the end of the day" comes back as "shuttin'-up time", "at this moment in time" is "abowt now, I reckon", "level playing field" is mowed down into "hent bin built on — yit" and

Rehearsals for the village production of Richard III; *the king has reservations about being buried under a car park in Leicester.*

"let's run this up the flagpole and see who salutes" transforms sweetly into "I hent got a clue woss a'gorn on!"

Perhaps you can see where I'm coming from when all is said and done. A good old coat of Norfolk paint can work wonders on the most confusing modern canvas. And it doesn't really hurt if you finish up overcome with emulsion.

Border bouts

"That's the old Shipmeadow over there where they used to have prize fights in the old days. Many a big turn-out with bare fists they've had on this island (on the Broads near Geldeston) in the Corinthian days. You see, if the Norfolk police came after them they could just hop over the river into Suffolk and if the Suffolk coppers were on their tracks, they just hopped back across the mill-stream into Norfolk!"

James Wentworth Day, *Portrait of the Broads,* 1967

9. MEDICINE

It can be extremely bad for your health to ask folk how they are. Far too many will take that as a cue to share a mounting pile of ailments, some of them yet to find a way into any medical handbook.

I have run the risk regularly on my Cromer rounds and even beyond if my poor old feet and aching shoulders aren't playing up too much. It came as a big relief when a local woman answered my casual inquiry about her general condition with an emphatic "Yew dunt want ter know!"

We've come a fair way since Norfolk village bulletins featured such rustic classics as "betterannerhebbin" and "wassanwotterwuz" (find a quiet corner and say them both out loud) in response to homely concerns regarding family and friends. Well, they made a change from "fair ter middlin'" or "my corns ent harf angry!"

It was remarkable how all sorts of afflictions sounded less painful or contagious when coated in broad Norfolk ... multiplication of the bowls, haricot veins, kangerene of the fut and wiper's darnse for a start.

People shivering were "all of a dudder". A boil or carbuncle turned into a "push". A troublesome cough transformed into a "tizzick". The "bronickle" brigade was out in force on a wintry morning.

Those in severe pain would exclaim "Blarst, that give me some clorth!" Those merely a bit off colour might mutter "I dunt feel up tew a sight". The vast majority, wary of pre-empting the overworked doctor, satisfied themselves by joining the queue anticipating treatment for Norfolk's most common complain ... "Suffin gorn abowt".

As a serial whimp who hears angels calling me home as soon as the nose clogs up, I seek a mite of solace in what our Norfolk ancestors went through in the poorly stakes without a chance to discover what daytime television is all about and the role it might play in hastening recovery.

Parson James Woodforde looked after his Weston Longville flock a few miles from Norwich and kept a comprehensive diary in the last part of the 18th century. He favoured port wine to keep sore throats at bay and dollops of rhubarb and ginger for just about everything else.

When he cut himself shaving he killed a small moth passing by and applied it to the mole "which instantaneously stopped the bleeding." He cured a nasty stye on the right eyelid by rubbing it with the tail of his black cat — although he admitted other cats' tails may have been as good.

When his servant Jack suffered another touch of the ague "I gave him a dram of gin at the beginning of the fit and pushed him headlong into a pond and ordered him to bed immediately. He was better after it ..."

The good parson's ailments multiplied on his final lap — he died on New Year's day in 1803 — and he appeared to suffer his own prolonged bout of "suffin' gorn abowt". He wrote "I am never well or ill and have at times strange feelings about me. Cold streams running over my shoulders and restless nights"

He could have done with a few chilblains to give him something new to worry about. A bit of toe-toasting in front of a log fire followed by bedtime bliss with a hot-water bottle could bring them on nicely.

I suffered constantly in the good old days when we had proper winters. Dipping them in a chamber-pot of fresh urine became a popular means of easing the pain, much preferred to other suggestions like rubbing onion juice, paraffin or turpentine on them or thrashing them with holly until they bled.

Running barefoot in the snow for five minutes also seemed a bit drastic although rumours that posh people dipped their chilblains in wine moved me to compromise with half a bottle of dandelion and burdock. My toes went a funny colour and I returned to taking pot luck.

Opposite: *Just a gentle squeeze will do it.*

Don't ask

Native wit and wisdom have long been used to put smart newcomers and strangers firmly in their place. The Norfolk response may be slow and deliberate but the old boy over the hedge invariably leaves an arrogant or sarcastic inquisitor on the ropes.

Here are examples of questions most commonly asked, complete with answers most generally provided ....

Have you lived here all your life?
No, not yit I hent.

Where does this road go to, my good man?
That dunt go nowhere. That stay here where thass wanted.

Why are the church bells ringing?
Cors someone's pullin' the rope.

Where are you going to, my good fellow?
I ent goin' nowhere ... I'm just a'cummin' back.

Are you in favour of progress?
Yis, as long as that dunt change noffin'.

Is that river good for fish?
Reckon that must be — I can't get any ter leave it.

Are you going to old Jacob's funeral?
No, an' I dunt reckon he'll come ter mine.

How would you like to be up there in that aeroplane?
Well, I shunt want ter be up there wi'owt it.

Have you had your eyes checked?
No, they've allus bin blue.

I suppose you have rung the Old Year out and the New Year in?
Yis, masrster, hundreds o' times.

An appealing picture from Cromer church tower.

Do you think the farmer could use me on the land?
No, they've got speshal stuff for that now.

How far apart should I plant these potatoes?
Harf in your garden — an' harf in mine.

Can I trust you to keep a secret?
Yis .. thass them I tell it to what carnt.

When your grandfather died, how much money did he leave?
Blarst, all of it ... you hev to!

10. CONFUSION

An occasional rush of letters to the Eastern Daily Press or lively debate on BBC Radio Norfolk reawakens countless arguments over the "correct" way to pronounce certain local place-names.

As one who lives near Elmerton, Hazeburrer, Munnsley, Porlin' and Webbun, I feel reasonably entitled to join in the fun — but you are not obliged to take my word for anything or anywhere along the way.

After all, my home town of Cromer comes out as "Crummier" on the computer spell-check. We get our own back by calling a nearby inland town Halt during the week and Howlt or Hewlt at the weekend where there are more posh people about.

They're the sort who enjoy a good blow on Hokum Beach and buy serious hats in Barnum Market. They don't get as far as Darsinum, Hunstan or Snettsum unless the charabanc takes a wrong turning on the road to Sarndringham.

Visitors and newcomers must take their share of the credit for confusing natives who knew where they stood when Vikings dropped in to set fire to signposts or ask for bawd and breakfast.

Happily, there's fair mileage yet in the likes of Alburgh, Guist, Hautbois, Postwick, Salle and Skeyton and a few choice abbreviations. Garblesham and Inglesthorpe top that list.

Some folk still talk fondly of Hindol — they are referring to Hindolveston — while Hunny can make it sticky going for strangers round the pretty parish of Hunworth. Then there's Sunny Hunny on the coast even when it might be raining in Hunstanton.

Long Stratton — not to be confused wtih Stratton Long, Stratton without any Straw or Rather Dumpy Stratton.

Norfolk's delight in dewin' diffrunt gives Gillingham a hard "G", unlike its much larger Kent counterpart. Colourful local corruptions not far from Cromer call up Nordrupps and Sudrupps.

In some cases older residents are best judges of the proper way to pronounce the name of the place where they live ... although there's no guarantee they will share that wisdom with outsiders. Nor are matters helped when polite inquiries about the identity of the oldest resident are met with a heartfelt "Oh, we hent got one now. He went an' died last week."

I have heard Cley veterans arguing vehemently over whether it rhymes with obey or deny. I've noticed gnarled natives discussing Hollem on the coast near Brancaster in one breath and Hoom Hale near Swaffham in the next.

I once went to Worrum, Wifton and Woodorlin' all in the same day. Scotter, Stanner and Study called the following week. I'm off to Belaugh tomorrow. Or is it Bylaugh?

You can't win. You can't lose. Take away all those pronunciation potholes from Norfolk's roads and we're left with the sort of blandscape any self-respecting Viking would ignore on village pillage rounds.

Here's another useful exercise to brighten up any Norfolk safari, finding new derivations for familiar names on the map. I've been playing this game ever since an old friend set the highest of standards with his version of how Saxlingham Nethergate came into being.

It was a wet day at harvest time on the farm. Workers were sent to the barn to take shelter and mend a big pile of corn sacks. They finished as the sun broke through.

The foreman asked the farmer where they store the fruits of their labours. The farm replied rather dismissively: "Sacks? Sling 'em near the gate."

While I turn my attention towards Houghton-on-the-Hill and Thorpe-next-Haddiscoe, here's a scholarly score compiled by Andrew Bealey of Holt. Note the meaty flavour:

Mousehold — standard technique in rodent wrestling.

Great Witchingham — Harry Potter's favourite cold meat.

Cromer - what a pious crow brought to the crib. His mates brought crow gold and crow frankincense.

Sheringham — not keeping all the ham to yourself.

King's Lynn — Slynn, England's forgotten king.

Aylsham — not real ale.

Dereham - ham that's not cheap.

Rackheath — to torture open shrubland.

Spixworth — utter the value of something.

Waveney — unorthodox gesture of farewell.

Wensum — what Ipswich Town seldom do.

Fakenham — pretending to be ham, but you're really a slice of corned beef.

Yarmouth — orifice just south of yar nose.

St Andrew's Hall — where St Andrew keeps everything.

Walsingham — ham dancing in the Viennese style.

Banham — militant group notoriously intolerant of cold pig meat.

Cow Tower — one who kow tows.

Blakeney — Chinaman damages joint between thigh and shinbone.

Norwich — what I've been all my life.

Wymondham — punch 'em hard in the solar plexus.

The mood at Wymondham Cross Keys became a bit ugly when we started the Wymondham gags. We then realised where the hostelry got its name and left quietly.

11. PATRONISED

I won't mention any hallowed names. To do so would run a clear risk of being tarred with the same moth-eaten brush as Norfolk's growing army of celebrity spotters.

In any case, it's far more fun to drop oblique little hints, spread a few extra spicy rumours and deliberately mislead, especially at the start of a new season on and around the Burnham Market catwalk.

This actress, that chef and the other talent show judge who thinks Walsingham Matilda is a real person ... they're the easy ones to lift out of a crowd and stick in the scrapbook of transient notoriety.

Recognising a lugworm bait digger from Brancaster Staithe, a chimney sweep from Thornham and a retired mole-catcher from the outskirts of Old Hunstanton demands so much more attention to detail on the part of those who find other people interesting.

As a general rule, these home-grown characters will preface most comments with "Cor, blarst me!" and pretend they don't have electricity in their tied cottages and as a consequence have no idea as to who or what comprises popular culture these days. They hum the theme tune from Dick Barton as a farewell gesture.

Another useful pointer for those trying to sort out wholesome wheat from chancy chaff is the good old Oxo tin held together by a giant elastic band. This refreshments receptacle contains Spam sandwiches, Norfolk shortcakes and coypu-flavoured crisps, a veritable spread on the hoof for natives who appreciate hard work when they see it.

Ironically, many refugees from various corners of tinsel town

Mardling masters Dick Bagnall-Oakley (left) and Ted Ellis get down to a serious nature study class. They are not having a picnic!

experience sudden pangs of envy when they encounter colourful indigenous remnants, just like capital journalist Clement Scott in the 1880s as he watched farm labourers gather in the corn harvest.

Never mind prickly sweat, long hours and poor wages ... "Laughter and song are heard all over the land, louder than the wind that bends the ripening corn or the sea that moans at the foot of the crumbling cliffs." Poppyland or Chelsea-on-Sea, flowery images can blossom to justify the invaders and mollify the invaded.

I recall a salutary tale passed on by Norfolk champion Dick Bagnall-Oakeley in the 1960s, a bit before the tourism stream turned into a

Life in Burnham Market before the rise of Chelsea on Sea.

waterfall. Even then, though, Dick realised it was too easy for traditional ways of rural life to be patronised or ridiculed.

A group of London friends informed the geography master, all-round sportsman, naturalist and dialect expert they were on their way to darkest Norfolk for a few days and would dearly love to tune into some genuine local characters in their natural environment. Dick emphasised he was not a sideshow organiser or "peasant shoot" enthusiast but could point the way to a pub where a band of good old boys regularly held court.

In constant demand on the after-dinner speaking circuit, Dick went off to sing for his supper and arranged to meet his metropolitan mates later that evening in the pub. He was greeted with mystified looks and exasperated cries of "We couldn't understand a single word!"

Dick admitted the dialect might offer a big challenge to the untrained ear but couldn't accept it was that unfathomable. He'd go to the bar for a half and linger long enough to discover what they were mardling about. He loitered, listened and laughed.

"I'm not surprised you couldn't make head or tail of 'em" confided Dick. "Them beggars are Polish!"

When I asked Dick if he'd planted those visitors in that village hostelry to teach smart chums a lesson he merely turned on an enigmatic smile reserved for puckish schoolteachers and hinted the world was getting smaller every day.

I have no doubt he could have called up any number of lugworm bait diggers, chimney sweeps and retired mole-catchers for the occasion but I know he preferred the cultural cross-fertilisation process to be as natural and beneficial as possible.

Remember, he taught pupils from all over the globe in his 25-year term at Gresham's School in Holt. Few left without a smattering of Norfolk dialect or at least an O-level in the undiluted glories of squit.

It may be time to revive the Bagnall-Oakeley primer or at least celebrate its uplifting spirit of sharing and enlightening. To this end, I warmly recommend a slight reversal of roles. Let the new age of spiritual twinning between Nelson's County and London begin with a parade of real tractors in Chelsea.

What a brave signal that would send to serial mockers like Jeremy Clarkson! And it ought to be followed up with evening lessons in Broad Norfolk for Hampstead's chattering classes and the opening of the Sinkers & Swimmers Dumpling Bar to help Westminster through any more recessions.

Well-lined retired mole-catchers from the outskirts of Old Hunstanton able to rent a tied apartment in the capital could catch a breath of home at the Mayfair Mardling Club while Norwich City season ticket holders with any capital left might invest and exchange yarns in Canary Weft, biggest store in London selling yellow and green wool.

Humble beginnings, perhaps, but such vital campaigns take time to stitch together.

Take care

The wisdom of long experience in the art of living does not take kindly to enthusiasts who would make sweeping changes. It wears them down so that in the end it is the innovators who are changed.

Bernard Dorman, *Norfolk*, 1972

12. INTEGRATION

I recall a dear old friend sending a poignant little note to the heart of my reputation as a fair-minded if rather entrenched sort of fellow: "Yesterday I completed 50 years as a Norfolk resident probationer. May I have my Norfolk passport now, please?"

I was flattered to be asked but had to confess such a prize was not in my gift. A full session of the Norfolk Passport Applications Committee sits at a secret destination round about midnight on a date to be fixed every November.

My friend's credentials as an appreciative and useful honorary citizen for half-a-century should have been strong enough to see him safely into the hallowed fold. I have known others get there in half the time.

This kind of good-natured exchange has punctuated my working life ever since I sought permission from the village elders to leave rural pastures and find out if the streets of Thetford were paved with gold.

In fact, they were lined with newcomers from London, the sort of discovery bound to set me up for any seismic sociological shocks to come along the local media highway. People still sidle up and apologise for not being lucky enough to be born in Norfolk or admit to slipping in the back door through marriage or other subtle ploys.

Like bribing border guards, deliberately getting lost around Wolterton, Quarles or Mautby or taking holy orders and volunteering to look after 15 country parishes. Bike provided.

As an ice-breaker for 25 years of Press Gang entertainment in local temples of culture, I requested at the outset of a show of hands by genuine natives bred and born thereabouts. They could then step out as interpreters and missionaries for the rest of the evening.

It helped put a fast-changing scene in perspective and engendered a new kind of togetherness before the bar reopened at half-time. Strangers had turned into friends although most still had to buy their own drinks.

Perhaps such efforts in the name of genuine integration have a fair way to go but it seems we still do far better than some.

Edward Storey, outstanding Fenland chronicler, moved from his spiritual flatlands to the foot of ancient hills in Wales well over a decade ago. We correspond regularly, exchanging views, news and valuable works of literature. He sent me a delightful little book with the mildly inflammatory title of "You're Not From Round Here, Are You?"

It's an *A to Z of Proper People and People From Off* by Roger Kite, a former university and college teacher of philosophy. It examines essential differences between Proper People, who have lived in the Welsh Marches for generations, and incomers, affectionately labelled People From Off.

Mr Kite flies in the face of most perceived wisdom connected with the search for harmony by suggesting someone from the other side of the world or just the next village must be treated exactly the same.

"It would seem that distance has nothing to do with offness. Despite any superficial similarities, People From Off are different. You are normal, they are not."

Clearly, the Welsh Marches bear little resemblance to the Norfolk Amblings, where I have observed a heartening brand of fresh tolerance in recent years. "Furriners" is often reserved now for folk from another county — especially Essex.

Meanwhile, Mr Kite charges on through his alphabet of antagonisms. Some will relish D is for Doing Things: "A common complaint from Proper People about People From Off is that they simply don't know how to do things. Now, clearly there are lots of things they do know to do.

"Such as managing offshore investments or knowing which golf club to use. So what are Proper People getting at?

"What they mean is that your typical Person From Off is of no use to them at all. He has no idea how to build a fence, trouse a hedge, deliver a calf, work a sheepdog, worm a horse, hang a gate or do anything else remotely useful to a Proper Person.

"So, grim though it is, the question has to be asked — just what are People From Off for?"

I assume my friend Edward Storey, a distinguished member of the People From Off department, is actively involved in useful missionary work in a hamlet scattered about lanes at the bottom of a hill in Powys.

Perhaps Mr Kite and like-minded colleagues should book a charabanc to Norfolk to sample a real taste of peaceful co-existence.

That is if they can get past passport control.

Way of life

Norfolk is not simply a word that describes a county. Norfolk also describes a language, a humour and a way of life. Spoken Norfolk has a stout and uniquely resistant quality and only people born in the county are able properly to penetrate it and repeat it with their own tongues. Just as their language, so also the people of Norfolk are tough, resistant and impenetrable. They guard to themselves the secrets of their language and of their humour. Yet humour there is in the Norfolk people, riotous and abundant. When you read Norfolk tales, remember that they are tales about a highly observant, subtle and recondite people. Therefore always think twice before you laugh at a Norfolk tale — the laugh might be on you!

Dick Bagnall-Oakeley, dialect expert, naturalist and teacher, 1974

13. AGGRAVATION

They need some convincing at Jifflers End (population 147) that Norfolk is rated one of the safest places in the country. A parish meeting has been called to discuss rural violence in light of a recent national survey suggesting such a gathering ought not to be necessary.

It is scheduled to start at 7.30pm next Thursday, provided the Golden Threads' afternoon session leaves the village hall standing. PC Whirl, whose beat also includes the larger settlements of Bosky Bottom, Clinker St Mawkin and Higglers Green, will be on the door.

Major Ernest Lummox-Hakes, whose family have ruled and riled the immediate locality in just about equal measure since 1468, and Martha Blunt, school dinner lady, crochet expert, chapel organist and Daniel O'Donnell devotee, are main instigators of a meeting described in a hastily-dispatched newsletter as "more than vital to the future of our historic community."

The Major, who lists the early adventures of Bulldog Drummond and Test cricket against countries we can beat as his main interests, blames a gradual decline in moral values since the retirement of Douglas Jardine and Mary Whitehouse for the upsurge of vandalism and violence.

He points to electrification of the railway line to London and abolition of rural district councils as contributory factors to "one of the darkest periods in our history since we lost the Empire" but says it is wrong to pin too much blame on the Yuppies on the new estate not far from his old estate. They don't ride motorbikes through his summer house or terrorise the peacocks with loud music.

The annual rabbit chase.

At Thursday's meeting the Major will demand the return of conscription as a first step along the road to recovery. "Look what the Grenadier Guards did for me and the Home Guard did for Tizzick, our faithful old retainer. There may be social divisions between us — he's certainly got more in the bank than me — but we can both look the world straight in the eye."

The Major stops short of deportation or restoration of the death penalty. "There's something rather final about that and it does fly in the face of our family motto about hanging fire until common sense calls."

Martha Blunt is sure all aggravation is tied up with diet. No chance of anyone wanting a punch-up after a steaming plateful of good ole Norfolk Swimmers made with Granny Lollop's famous dumpling recipe, including brandy, sherry and Sanatogen.

She accepts the spirit of conflict is not confined to the younger set although she could hardly believe reports of a nasty incident at the post office and store last pension day. Evidently, it all began when the lady with blue hair nudged the lady with orange hair. The brave man with no hair was threatened by both as he tried to act as peacemaker.

Two windows broken, the doorbell silenced for the first time in living memory as it came down in the jostling, the ice cream sign torn from its hinges and five tins of special-offer peas badly dented.

It is believed Blue Hair had claimed Swaffham Market was held on a Tuesday. Orange Hair swore it was a Thursday. No Hair voted for

Saturday because he used to live at North Pickenham before it became too crowded.

Police were called and only after earnest pleas by postmistress Grace Yellums did they agree not to take away for forensic tests three shooting sticks, two walking frames, a dozen mothballs and a top set of false teeth as offensive weapons thought to have been used in making an affray.

Jifflers End, therefore, must brace itself for a spell of soul-searching, especially if the parish is to give the lead to others suffering breakdowns in law and order. Those who genuinely care are unanimous in their desire to bring back the good old days and the good old ways.

Hunting, shooting, beating, poaching, badger-baiting, coursing, ferreting, bare-knuckle fighting, ripping out hedges — all gentlemanly pursuits in their time.

The charming rustic ritual of chasing rabbits as they scatter from the last bit of corn to be cut. The character-building fun of stoning lads from nearby villages as they dare to woo your local mawthers.

The pure joy of a local sporting derby boiling up into a full-scale battle. The sheer thrill of chasing off anyone who comes within a mile of plumpest blackberries on your patch. The quaintness of seeing someone you know taking a breather in the stocks on the village green or enjoying a late-night dip in the duck pond.

It is only when such long-lost cornerstones of country living are restored to the crumbling fabric of our smaller communities that the quality of rural life will take a turn for the better.

Jifflers End village hall must be packed next Thursday evening.

Hearty types

The Norfolk people are quick and smart in their motions and in their speaking. Very neat and trim in all their farming concerns and very skilful. Great admiration for this county of excellent farmers and hearty, open and spirited men.

William Cobbett, *Rural Rides*, 1821

14. BIKE-HOLDING

Granny Biffin, by a country mile Bronickle End's oldest and wisest indigenous remnant, is thrilled to find the ancient Norfolk sport of bike-holding back in the limelight.

"It suffered a bit of slow puncture when wartime rules and regulations put paid to so many wholesome pastimes, especially as Muckwash Magna Home Guard commandeered all our machines for manoeuvres, but this area long remained a stronghold for a noble and community-welding art" she told me as we sipped elderberry tea in her cosy little cottage.

Fond of calling herself a recycled teenager, this affable rural sage is quick to point out how big a role the humble bike played in the social and working lives of countless country folk throughout much of the 20th century. Fresh air and exercise went with pushing, pedalling, puffing, posing — and holding.

"It was very fashionable on Sunday afternoons in summer for local lads to try to impress local mawthers with the way they handled a bicycle. Some settled for a firm grip on the handlebars and a straight-ahead look while others tried their luck with a cavalier slouch over the seat and a saucy smile. A few fiddled with the bell or tweaked the tyres.

"An essential part of the rustic courtship ritual and we gals knew that months or even years of dressing up in our go-to-meeting-clothes for these outdoor sessions could be rewarded with what became known around here as The Magic Saddlebag Moment."

She knew I was hooked and so allowed herself a lengthy pause to build

Mass bike-holding display at Fakenham in 1897.

more anticipation. A broad smile dared me to question the validity of her report from the front line. "Any boy certain of a girl's close interest after a series of meetings, possibly without any words being exchanged, would dart to the rear of his machine to produce flowers, sweets, a book of poems or even a carbide lamp as a token of undying affection."

That action was strong enough to allow the young people to cycle together in and around the immediate area without any harassment from those still sizing up their options or saving up for a telling gift. Indeed, it carried the strongest of hints that an official engagement was not far round the corner.

I asked Granny Biffin if girls ever took the initiative in these bike-holding adventures and rode or walked out to set hearts a'fluttering with their own brand of subtle enticement. She replied it was hardly ladylike to pursue such a course — although a Puckaterry Parva woman of indeterminate years and doubtful virtue had set tongues wagging in the early 1930s.

"She would strike a provocative pose near the crossroads, holding her bike with one hand and extending the other with a beckoning finger to all male passers-by. It must have worked 'cos she married the squire's oldest son and travelled for the rest of her life in a smart car."

What about official bike-holding competitions when points rather than hearts were at stake? Yes, there were prestigious events on Celandine Meadow behind Farmer Dunnock's Barn forming part of the Whit Monday Sporting Extravaganza.

The Samphire Sisters from Little Coughwort dominated their section throughout the 1920s, Sarah excelling in the general deportment and outstanding brakes class while Sukey left her rivals trailing when it came to pristine mudguards and perfect tyre pressure.

"I took part just the once on my trusty old steed but dropped vital points for a broken bell, loose spoke, wobbly seat and signs of spilt milk in the front basket. But I did get a highly commended certificate for a tight chain" reminisced my rural correspondent.

Apparently, the male contests tended to degenerate rather speedily into heated arguments over biased judging by leading exponents of the art who encouraged their sons to carry on a proud family tradition.

Matters came to a head in 1929 when Winston Burke from Muckwash Magna won the Burke Trophy for All-Round Composure for the ninth successive year. His father, Obadiah Burke, headed the examining panel on each occasion while his uncle, Elijah, had presented the cup for competition to mark the end of international hostilities in 1918.

"There were too many Burkes taking the whole thing far too seriously but a new generation brought a fresh approach to matters after the last war. The scoring system was simplified for a start so every family represented could take part" said Granny Biffin.

The future? "People must get fed up eventually with all those cars. Bike-holding will blossom again. Long live the village pump!"

A quiet day at the pump.

15. ECCENTRIC

I've been ambling along Cromer seafront wondering out loud why they didn't regenerate me while they were about it.

Much easier to get away with that sort of eccentric behaviour in November when most of the people you're likely to bump into are either doing the same or are fully at ease with those who do.

Pier and promenade provide a sort of "safe house" from boring matters like where the next supermarket will spring up on the outskirts of town, when someone resembling a traffic warden may reappear on the streets and why so many shoppers have to ring home to find out what colour wrapping paper they want.

I suppose Sunday school outings to Hunstanton and Great Yarmouth in the 1950s nurtured that spirit of escapism as we sniffed annual rations of ozone, rejuvenated toes in sea and sand, made friends with donkeys instead of rounding up cows and invested nearly a shilling in slot machines to win a Woodbine.

Free for a day from the shackles of rural convention, we could ignore big-family commandments such as "Don't spend all your pennies in one go" and "Thou shalt not show thyself up by turning green along the Golden Mile after a crafty fag by the boating lake."

Even then, I noticed how many sensible older folk just sat and watched the ebb and flow of holiday humanity searching for the next thrill, another excuse to be a bit more daring than usual, a rare chance to wear a silly hat and plunder a menu of candy floss, toffee apples and doughnuts. With fish and chips for afters.

Cromer 80 years BS (Before Skipper). I continue to tread these paths but haven't met any Empresses.

I never sampled the seaside in winter until the mid-1960s when press reporting rounds took me back to Yarmouth as icy winds growled, angry waves roared and figures outside the waxworks museum wanted to huddle together for a spot of warmth.

So began a long-term relationship, occasionally bordering on flirtation with melancholy, between my more thoughtful moods and Norfolk's edge at its rawest.

As an honorary Crab since 1988, I have moaned about summer excesses like any self-respecting free spirit capable of seeing tourists as "space invaders" and then wallowed in winter expanses of time and room to ponder and roam.

That can hardly warrant a "selfish" vote, especially from those determined to shove an all-year-round tourism bandwagon into the teeth of fiercest gales, be they economic or straight off the North Sea.

It takes a special kind of masochist to yell "Welcome to Poppyland!" and do the job for them as a solo act entertaining rigor mortis on the end of Cromer Pier in the bleakest of mid-winters. I await my due reward.

Most glowing tributes to Cromer's enduring charms come from the summer pens of literary callers. Compton Mackenzie, famous for his novel *Whisky Galore*, is a prime example of someone who never knew the other side of the town's character.

He only soaked up the sun and mixed with the best, recalling in his autobiography how as a four-year-old in 1887 he found himself seated on the beach next to a "tall and beautiful lady" with heavily plaited dark hair and a notebook on her knee. She turned out to be the Empress of Austria.

Young Compton loved the surrounding countryside, fields of poppies and ox-eyed daisies which "always seemed to be overflowing from behind into the little seaside town" and the smell of honeysuckle in the July dusk "mingling its sweetness with the salty air."

Whether she visited or not, novelist Elizabeth Gaskell also managed an outstanding public relations role in North and South, published in 1855. She sent her contemplative heroine Margaret Hale to Cromer for a rest-cure. It appears to have worked:

"She used to sit long hours upon the beach, gazing intently on the waves as they chafed with perpetual motion against the pebbly shore — or she looked out upon the more distant heave and sparkle against the sky, and heard, without being conscious of hearing, the eternal psalm, which went up continually. She was soothed without knowing how or why."

A choppy sea at Cromer.

Now, wouldn't it have been far more intriguing to see how young Compton, the jotting Empress and pensive Margaret coped with a few of them lazy old winds from the Arctic turning parasols inside out and rendering blue the most fashionable of seafront colours?

I pass a beach hut called The Shud and realise this is modern Norfolk catering for modern tastes. Boards to protect against vandalism and weather are going up all along our coast. Gulls decry the end of their takeaway season.

A couple of beachcombers melt into crouching shadows while festive lights burn in hotel windows above. A woman with a dog tugging her along scampers past as if bent on beating a dusky deadline.

There are times when I am soothed by these surroundings without really knowing how or why. I may hear the eternal psalm without catching all the words. Gazing at waves could be the perfect antidote to shopping.

I am certain, however, that our seaside in winter is good for the soul ... even if it has to be wrapped in several extra layers.

Such variety

All England may be carved out of Norfolk, represented therein not only to the kind but degree itself. Here are fens and heaths, and light and deep, and sand and clay ground, and meadows and pastures, and arable and woody, and (generally) woodless land; so grateful is this shire with the variety thereof. Thus, as in many men, through perchance this or that part may justly be cavilled at, yet all put together complete a proper person; so Norfolk, collectively taken, hath a sufficient result of pleasure and profit, that being supplied in one part which is defective in another.

Thomas Fuller, *Worthies of England*, 1662

16. ESCAPISM

One of Norfolk's most enduring and endearing habits is to encourage the more daring among us to push routine aside and make life up on the hoof for a few golden hours.

I served a useful apprenticeship at grammar school when single algebra, double biology and treble physics tended to pall on sultry days made for cricket, a good book on the boundary or a crisis meeting of skiffle group candidates still looking for a tea chest.

I knew many a genius had emerged from long hours of devotion to gazing out of the window or, in more subtle mode, staring straight at the teacher as if hanging on every word instead of seeing and hearing absolutely nothing for up to 30 minutes at a time.

Yes, I did occasionally get caught napping "somewhere else, boy!" when asked about properties of certain numbers, the frog's reproductive system or why the balance of the ball bearing had been disturbed. But no amount of embarrassment or detention could dilute the sheer joy of going absent while still being there.

I took this useful form of escapism into less dangerous waters when preachers put down anchors for Sunday afternoon and evening eternity in our village chapel. At least they didn't stop suddenly, thump the pulpit, point at my miles-away face and ask why Ahab was so anxious to acquire Naboth's vineyard, how to spell Deuteronomy or to name the last book in the Old Testament. (In case you don't know, it's Malachi).

Then followed a natural progression into surrounding lanes and lokes with a bike, sandwiches and voyages to the other side of the world

Not content with Hoveton and Coltishall, a bus in Wroxham heads for Newmarket and London.

at least five miles away. Free to sing like David Whitfield, whistle like Ronnie Ronalde, pop over to Lord's and make up a highly favourable score for England's openers and pretend to get lost when it was time to head home and help in the garden.

A lengthy career in the media afforded plenty of opportunities to take my disappearing act to new levels, especially as a press reporter at boring dinners or annual meetings when I had the foresight to ask rambling speakers for copies of their speeches beforehand.

Most were flattered to be asked, politicians in particular as they added up potential column inches, while those who gave me questioning looks soon handed over the goods when I confessed to a rather dodgy shorthand system.

As they droned on like generations of teachers, preachers and parents before them, I trusted them to stick to the script while I conjured up another masterful chapter for that best-selling Norfolk novel starring a man of agricultural property with romantic inclinations. I never did finish The Farmer Sutra.

I also cultivated a very useful mime act at the back of the room when forced to attend and pay attention at "vital intelligence" meetings called by the BBC to give important people from London the chance to discover Norfolk and issue rousing cries of "Carry on, chaps and chapesses!"

I cupped a hand to my ear in exaggerated fashion at every utterance of "I hear what you say", put an imaginary telescope to my eye on being assured "I see where you're coming from" and saluted firmly but politely whenever a brave new idea went up the flagpole.

Where was I? Oh yes, making life up on the hoof just for the fun of it. After a long cold winter, a warm sun brought me out in a puckish rash the other morning. We hadn't played "take the next turning right" or "let's see what is down here" since the boys left home.

Thankfully, my wife saw fit to indulge an old man's thinly-disguised passion for the past as daffodils and primroses, daisies and dandelions paved the way through Holt into that surprisingly undulating countryside around Thornage.

I wanted reminders of good-looking villages nestling in their own little comfort zones far from the madding development crowd. Brinton and Sharrington fitted the opening bill perfectly and we savoured some of their gentle self-sufficiency in parish churches and churchyards full of light and life.

Diversions galore brought the chance to cross the main Holt-Fakenham road to rediscover the charms of Bale, Field Dalling and Langham before marshes called to say it might be a good idea to drop in now for fresh air and space on the eve of a new holiday rush.

There was an air of surrender gathering over Stiffkey as that narrow and twisty through road apologised yet again to a stream of vehicles for not being modern enough to take the growing load. I wonder how many locals or second homers bother to try to get to the other side in summer.

We finished part one of our impromptu safari in a Wells bookshop comparing the bitter winds of a lingering winter. I put up a decent case for Cromer built on numbing evidence from lifelong residents but a couple of Staithe Street stalwarts claimed the crown for Wells with "five coats colder than usual" headlines.

I urged the wife to take the Boadicea Trail home. She thought I was making that up. "No," I insisted, "it's the Icenic Route."

17. LAUGHTER

Welcome to the official Norfolk launch of LAUGH — Life's About Upholding Good Humour.

Yes, I realise it's a dodgy time to demand grins ahead of groans, chuckles before chagrin, mirth instead of misery. But just recall what made this "dew diffrunt" empire how it is today. Be proud and join without delay or annual subscription.

I appreciate that analysing humour is like dissecting a frog — few people are interested and the frog dies — but even Jane Austen, that darling of the throwaway line at breakfast, reminds us: "For what do we live but to make sport of our neighbours, and laugh at them in our turn?"

Or to put it the Norfolk way, you might as well take the juice out of yourself now and again because everyone else does. Add the two together and there's a perfect survival package for at least a year of bobbing around in a leaky bathtub on a boiling sea of uncertainty.

No, this isn't a thin excuse to trot out a few more of my favourite local yarns. It's a heartfelt plea for the county that gave the nation Nelson, Kett, Hansard, Walpole, Edrich, proper dumplings and the Singing Postman to lead the way in smiling in the face of adversity.

What Norfolk does today might well dictate the shape and size of British resistance thereafter. We need a dash or two of the old Dunkirk spirit... and remember there is a Dunkirk on the Norfolk coast as well.

Opposite: A somewhat eccentric bike-holding pose — our man has forgotten the basic rule.

Where to start? Well, we all face stiff challenges on our daily rounds, bumping into poor folk whose faces appear frozen in a permanent state of grumpiness. A few may fade away beyond redemption, especially men in shops who would rather be anywhere else, but most can be lured back to the funny side of the street with a light-hearted insult like: "Please don't go. I want to forget you exactly as you are."

It's important not to let personal preferences or prejudices place obstacles in the path of this campaign to put fun back into Fundenhall, laughs back into Belaugh and Bylaugh and joy back into Happisburgh.

Stripes at Happisburgh.

For example, it can no longer be reasonable to dismiss mobile phone users in public places as preening, prodding, prattling posers. An ever-diminishing band of technophobes owe it to a forgiving society to encourage cheers and applause for colourful antics advertising the march of rich progress during a period of grim austerity.

Same goes for wags who like to text and chat while driving along our information superhighway. They ought to be saluted with at least a broad smile for demonstrating such dexterity under pressure, although care has to be taken not to distract them too much at peak times, especially if there are children on board.

Another area in sore need of a new brand of cheerful tolerance is television comedy. We can't live on Dad's Army, Bilko, Hancock, Porridge and Newsnight.

An ever-shrinking rump of media traditionalists, brought up on the Daily Herald and Brains Trust, must now accept that "cutting edge", "groundbreaking" and "in-your-face" are not bywords for crude, malevolent and unaccountable.

Cultural champions such as Jeremy Clarkson, Graham Norton and Alan Partridge ought to be lauded, particularly when they do Norfolk the honour of reminding the rest of the world it still exists. If they do it with a roguish tongue, just bear in mind how many sensitive and intelligent people will pay us a visit to see if what they say is true. The sort of economic spin-off money cannot buy and tourism chiefs dare not try.

Norfolk's ability to laugh at itself, except in very rare cases when national drama productions playfully confuse it with Devon, Dorset or Somerset, will continue to inspire other parts of the country to be less precious about image and homespun idiosyncrasies.

"Well, they wouldn't make all that fuss in Norfolk about a vicar putting ferrets down his trousers....."

I will set the tone with a local yarn from Barry Beales. His father Ted was a policeman stationed at Docking. One of his duties was to check on reports of after-hours drinking.

The Norfolk Hero pub in Stanhoe figured on Ted's visiting list. The "raid" went ahead and one of Ted's tasks was to note what drinks customers had in front of them. He came to a little chap in the corner.

"What are you drinking?" asked Ted.

The customer looked up and replied drily: "Thanks very much, Ted. I'll have a small brown."

Firm grip of Norfolk law in the countryside.

18. SHOPPING

My aversion to shopping, and to vast numbers of miserable moochers who treat it as a perfect excuse to advertise the nation's shortcomings, stretches well past that Yuletide panic launched in late August.

I can't take it seriously much beyond books, bloaters, liquorice allsorts and those display folder thingys with about 30 see-through pockets for vital intelligence of little use to enemies outside Norfolk's ethnic minority.

Perhaps my check-out chutzpah reached an unsustainable peak several years ago when a sudden downpour forced me to take refuge in a large city store. I dripped and dawdled until a smart young man came up and asked if he might help.

"Where's stationery these days?" I blurted out the first thing to enter my damp head. "Oh, stationery's moved, sir, over there next to newspapers and magazines. Were you after anything in particular?" Well, no, I'd just come in from the rain.

Suddenly, a classroom spelling bee from about 1954 came buzzing down a nearby escalator to camouflage my indolence.

"But it can't move if it's stationary" I smirked, wondering if he would notice how craftily I'd changed the eighth letter to an "a".

"Sorry, sir, but stationery has been moved over there next to newspapers and magazines" he repeated with quiet determination to maintain the eighth letter as an "e".

Opposite: *A shop with self-holding bicycles.*

RANDALL
WATCHMAKER
GAS ENGINEER
ELECTRICIAN &c
CYCLES

I didn't push my luck and ask if the books department stocked a little number called You Can't Win Them All. "Thanks for your help" I lied and went loitering towards the perfume counter.

An exasperating episode from the early 1970s left me similarly concerned about the future of mankind. The fact I was on the way to Millwall for a football match had surprisingly little to do with those Saturday afternoon misgivings.

I mounted a bus with a youthful reporting colleague about two miles from the ground. "Dogs must be carried" announced a notice at the front of stairs to the top deck. Time for a lead role in Spot The Provincial.

"Go and tell the conductor we're very sorry, but we haven't got a dog" I whispered. My young friend stared at the notice, stared at me, stared at the conductor and then repeated the exercise in exactly the same order.

I waited for a flicker of a smile, a cheery word of reproach, a knowing nudge in the ribs, a gentle whoof of appreciation. None there came, so I paid both fares, told the conductor we'd try to be more canine-friendly next time and prepared for walkies to welcoming Cold Blow Lane.

My father enjoyed better luck when he told our village parson a good one when I was too young to appreciate high-class satire prepared and packaged in a respected mid-Norfolk emporium.

Apparently, my mother had taken me to the Kingston & Hurn grocery store on her weekly mission by bus into Dereham for family provisions and placed me tidily on the counter while filling her bags. The parson chortled heartily as father completed the story with exaggerated bluster:

"Blarst if that boy didn't slip tew close ter the bearcun slicer — an' they got a little behind wi' thar orders!"

I couldn't remember the incident now causing such mirth but gladly accepted a consoling pat on the head from a tickled reverend. He muttered something about feeding the five thousand, stirred his tea and guffawed again.

Frankly, I cannot recall much drama or humour on the shop floor since that divine interlude.

Opposite: If you find me wandering in Cromer, I appreciate help with shopping.

There was a massive breakthrough last week when I returned home with the correct non-stick scouring pads and fabric conditioner concentrate — I thought that last word was a subtle instruction to show a bit more attention than usual— but plans for a big celebration are on hold.

My wife discovered I had wheedled sympathy and support from two kind women in Cromer town centre shops with my trademark helpless looks and forlorn shrugs. They could have been working undercover for Shelfassured, Help the Anguished or Kaos (Keep Amateurs Out of Shops) but simple compassion stamped my ration book.

Some of my long-term disenchantment with the retail world stems from confusing lines in windows. I spotted "Big Sale. Last Week" and thought how easy to always miss it. This was just rubbing it in.

Only a good laugh offers hope for the future. Assistants must react positively when they ask if you've got a list and you reply, no, that's the way you always stand.

Then you can pitch for a real winner from the Tommy Cooper Guide to Happy Shopping by going to the butcher's and betting him 50 quid he can't reach meat off the top shelf.

He'll play the game and reply: "No, the steaks are too high."

The big three

Let any stranger find me out so pleasant a county, such good ways, large heaths, three such places as Norwich, Yarmouth and Lynn in any county in England, and I'll be once again a vagabond and visit them.

Sir Thomas Browne, 17th century settler

Good roads

The roads in this county afford the farmer a very great advantage over many other parts of England, being free from sloughs in all parts (except the marshes) and though the soil is sandy, it resists the pressure of the wheels at a small distance from the surface, and the ruts are kept shallow at a very little expense; and after the longest and hardest rain, become dry and pleasant in a few days; so that I may venture to say that the roads are better in their natural state than in almost any other country; so good that no turnpike was thought of in Norfolk, till they become common in most other parts ...

Nathaniel Kent, *Agricultural Survey of Norfolk*, 1796

Awareness

Norfolk's population is now one of the fastest growing in the United Kingdom. Although this brings much-needed investment to what has been a rural backwater, it is all the more important that the awareness of the past should be the basis of planning for the future.

Susanna Wade Martins, *Norfolk — A Changing Countryside*, 1988

Into our midst

Strangers who come into our midst are inclined to treat us either with benevolent condescension or with undisguised superciliousness — and then expect us to acclaim them as saviours and the harbingers of civilisation.

H J Harcourt, *Norfolk Magazine*, 1948

Lightning Source UK Ltd.
Milton Keynes UK
UKHW021815010519
341945UK00002B/42/P

9 781909 796126